CAN YOU
BECOME A
SOCIAL MEDIA
INFLUENCER?

BY ERIC BRAUN

CAPSTONE PRESS
a capstone imprint

Published by Capstone Press, an imprint of Capstone.
1710 Roe Crest Drive
North Mankato, Minnesota 56003
capstonepub.com

Library of Congress Cataloging-in-Publication Data
Names: Braun, Eric, 1971- author.
Title: Can you become a social media influencer? : an interactive adventure / by Eric Braun. Description: North Mankato, Minnesota : Capstone Press, [2022] | Series: You choose: chasing fame and fortune | Includes bibliographical references. | Audience: Ages 8-12 | Audience: Grades 4-6 | Summary: "Do you want to make social media your microphone to the world? Maybe you're a trendsetter or a social justice leader. Now is your chance to set out on a path to social media domination. Face real-life choices that will help you learn about marketing, messaging, and what it takes to make it as a social media star."— Provided by publisher.
Identifiers: LCCN 2021042156 | ISBN 9781663959003 (hardcover) | ISBN 9781666323993 (paperback) | ISBN 9781666324006 (pdf)
Subjects: LCSH: Online social networks—Juvenile literature. | Social media—Juvenile literature. | Internet personalities—Juvenile literature. | Social influence—Juvenile literature. | Video blogs—Juvenile literature.
Classification: LCC HM742 .B737 2022 | DDC 302.23/1—dc23
LC record available at https://lccn.loc.gov/2021042156

Editorial Credits
Editor: Mandy Robbins; Designer: Heidi Thompson; Media Researchers: Jo Miller and Pam Mitsakos; Production Specialist: Tori Abraham

Photo Credits
Getty Images: RicardoImagen, 53; Shutterstock: 13_Phunkod, 13, Antonio Guillem, 47, Apollofoto, 75, Black Creator 24, Cover (right), Dmytrenko Vlad, 97, fizkes, 37, Freeograph, 19, GalacticDreamer, 83, Jacob Lund, 10, Natalia Toropova, Cover (left), Rawpixel.com, 29, Roman Samborskyi, 88, Sergey Peterman, 61, ThatStockCompany, 34, wavebreakmedia, 100, zealous, 41

Design Elements: Shutterstock: koltsovserezha, Nina_FOX, Southern Wind, Vasya Kobelev

All internet sites appearing in back matter were available and accurate when this book was sent to press.

Printed and bound in the USA. PO4608

TABLE OF CONTENTS

MAKING IT
BIG!

YOU have big dreams. You want the fame. You want the fortune. And you're willing to do whatever it takes to make your dream come true. But it's never a straight shot to the top, especially when it comes to the quickly changing trends on social media. Discover if you have what it takes to find fame and fortune as a social media influencer.

• Turn the page.

The first chapter sets the scene. Then you choose which path to read. Follow the directions at the bottom of each page. The choices you make will change your outcome. After you finish one path, go back and read the others for more adventures.

• Turn the page to begin your adventure.

YOU CHOOSE
THE PATH YOU TAKE TO BECOME A
SOCIAL MEDIA INFLUENCER.

ATTENTION
PLEASE!

YOU love social media. Sharing photos, posting videos, or just chatting—you love it all. You enjoy staying in touch with friends and family. You like spreading jokes, good news, and adorable images. You love sharing your thoughts and getting smart, witty, thoughtful replies. You love sharing your feelings and feeling the love in return.

• Turn the page.

Maybe your favorite thing about social media is feeling like you always know what's going on. What are your friends doing? What's in style? What are celebrities and trendsetters talking about? You feel like you're at the center of it all, soaking in the culture. Sometimes you even help create a little culture with your own content.

You are an impressive content creator. Compared to most noncelebrities, you're popular online. Plenty of people follow your feeds. They look forward to your posts. You regularly interact with people all over the world. You're entertaining. You're thoughtful. People say they trust your taste in brands.

Okay, you're not famous or anything. Not yet. But maybe you could be. Maybe you could earn a living as a social media figure. Maybe you'll even be a STAR!

You mention this idea to a couple friends. They ask you what kind of influencer you want to be. "You could do fashion and beauty," Lexi says. "Everyone knows you have great fashion sense. You could give advice and get free products. It would be fun!"

• Turn the page.

"You should do comedy!" Robert says. "You crack me up all the time. We could help you do skits and stuff. I follow tons of funny influencers. Some of them have millions of followers."

These are both great ideas. You also like playing music and have dreamed of making it as a performer. Any one of these ideas could be a good choice for you. Which do you choose?

- To try to be a fashion and beauty icon, turn to page 15.
- To try to build a comedy channel, turn to page 45.
- To try being a musician and performer, turn to page 77.

SKIN DEEP?

You believe that beauty is about more than looking good on the outside. Feeling good about yourself is an important part of self-image. You want to help make that a bigger part of the fashion and beauty world. You choose to focus on this area so you can help people show off their best, most positive, beautiful side.

Your friends often turn to you for tips. Even your mom and some of her friends seek your advice on occasion.

• Turn the page.

You ask your loyal Instagram followers to spread the word about you. You start posting several times a day, so when new followers check you out, they will find lots of fresh content. You also study successful influencers. What do they do well that you could learn from?

The best influencers are active on multiple platforms. They refer people from one platform to the others. Influencers expand on ideas in videos that they show in photos in other places. That way they find followers on every platform.

Your Instagram profile is going strong. You start making TikTok videos too. But in order to take this to the next level, you need to branch out to another platform. Do you start blogging or do you start doing how-to videos on YouTube?

- To start blogging, go to page 17.
- To start doing videos, turn to page 19.

Blogging can be a good way to broaden your audience. Writing gives your content more depth than it can have with images and videos.

Your first blog post is about picking Instagram filters when you're outside on a sunny day. You promote it on Instagram and TikTok. Many of your followers share it as well. You follow that post with fun posts about body piercings, retro hairstyles, and ice cream—because everyone deserves a treat now and then. You include lots of photos of yourself.

Your positive voice really shines through. You get comments from readers telling you you're funny, smart, and promote a positive body image. Soon, your blog has almost as many subscribers as you have Instagram or TikTok followers.

• Turn the page.

Then something disturbing happens. You are coming out of a grocery store when some older guy starts yelling at you. He says your spikey, green-dyed hair is ugly. "Don't you want to look like a lady?" he says.

It was a scary situation. You were alone, and he was much bigger. Once you get home, you are angry. You bang out a post about this man. "My hair, my choice!" you write near the end of the post.

People love the post and share it widely. Suddenly, your following spikes. You get lots of encouragement from people who agree with you. You also get some hateful comments from people defending the guy. Should you write another post about the same topic? You might be able to grow your following even more. On the other hand, it's no fun getting hate messages.

- To write another post about the issue, turn to page 22.
- To move on to another topic, turn to page 24.

If there's one thing you know from TikTok, it's that people love videos. And why not? Videos are fun. They're an easy way to learn things and be entertained at the same time. And for fashion and beauty, videos are a perfect platform.

• Turn the page.

You and Lexi brainstorm ideas for videos. She helps you with writing material, staging sets, working a camera, and editing. She even appears with you in some of the videos. When she's on screen with you, the two of you laugh a lot. You compare your opinions on beauty and fashion trends and try different products. Even when you disagree, you have a good time. People leave comments saying that you two make a good team.

One day you're planning to shoot a video about a new brand of yoga apparel. That's when you notice that you have a huge zit right on the tip of your nose. It's red. It's painful. And it is not easy to hide. You decide to put off shooting the video for a few days, until it goes away. But instead, you get two more zits. Then two more! This is one serious breakout.

"You have to do a video about your zits!" Lexi says. "People will love it!"

"This is supposed to be a beauty channel," you tell her. "I can't put up a bunch of images of me that don't look good."

"I'm telling you," Lexi says, "people are going to love it. It shows you're real."

- To post about your acne, turn to page 26.
- If there is no way you are posting about your acne, turn to page 28.

Outrage sells. Anger attracts clicks. You want to grow your audience. You'd be silly not to write a follow-up post about the man who yelled at you.

You dashed off your first post quickly, while you were still mad. This time, you are more thoughtful. You talk about typical beauty standards and common expectations. You also discuss why so many people think it's okay to judge one another.

This post attracts an even bigger response than the first one. You are interviewed by a well-known national women's magazine. All of your social media accounts blow up. You're contacted by a hair dye company. They want you to talk about their products on social media, and they'll pay you to do it! You take the deal. Then you get another deal from a jeans brand. You are starting to make good money from your social media.

There's a makeup brand that you often use. Their image is an ideal match for you—rebellious and smart. You think you would be a great influencer to represent them. It would also mean good money and free makeup for you.

Should you contact them about a partnership? You are hot now. This might be the right time. On the other hand, maybe you should wait until you have a bigger following. Then you can ask them for more money. They'd also be more likely to say yes.

- To contact them now, turn to page 30.
- To wait until you have more followers, turn to page 32.

The angry post was a nice way to get some attention, but it's time to move on. There are a few popular topics that are important to you, and you choose to write about organic skincare. A celebrity recently commented that she is no longer using a particular makeup line after realizing they use certain chemicals. You write a thoughtful post about why these chemicals are bad for both people and the environment. You mention some brands you prefer. Then you include some fab photos of yourself applying your favorite shade of lipstick.

The post gets shared a lot—almost as much as the angry post. People keep commenting on how great you look. So you do more posts giving makeup tips. Your audience is growing, when a friend of your friend Robert contacts you. Her name is Anna, and she wants to be your manager. She has helped a few other influencers grow, but nobody huge.

You do need a manager. Brainstorming material and communicating with brands is a lot of work. You also need someone to negotiate advertising packages for you. Robert says Anna is legit. Do you take a chance on this relatively unknown stranger? Or do you try to find a more experienced manager?

- To take a chance with Anna, turn to page 34.
- To hire a more experienced manager, turn to page 36.

"All right," you tell Lexi, "let's do it. I hope you're right."

At the beginning of the video, you and Lexi pretend that you're going to talk about something very serious: cosmetic testing on animals. But Lexi pretends to get distracted by your acne. She makes a joke, you make another joke, and soon you are bantering about zits. You talk about all the solutions you have tried, and how hard it is to battle those tenacious little things. You edit the video with a few funny sound effects—*boing,* there's another zit!—and post it on your channel. You cross post on Instagram and TikTok, add the hashtag #zitlifeisreallife, and sit back and wait.

People tell you that you're brave and real. They admire you for sharing your personal struggles. You gain many new followers. You even record another video about zits to follow up.

Meanwhile, Lexi starts doing her own beauty posts. Her follower count starts to rise too. She asks you to be a guest on a series of videos on her channel. Influencers do this type of thing all the time to get crossover followers. Typically it's a win for both parties. But what if people like her more than you? What if your subscribers start watching her instead?

- To do a video on Lexi's channel, turn to page 38.
- To turn her down, turn to page 39.

You just can't risk showing yourself with that breakout. You decide to wait until your skin clears up. In the meantime, you make a video about sunsets and nature shots. When you appear in the videos, you carefully hide your pimples.

The videos come off as weird. People wonder why you are posting about nature when you're supposed to be a fashion and beauty influencer. "Why is she always holding her hand over her nose like that?" someone writes in the comments.

People are losing interest in your channel. You need to recapture their attention. When your skin clears up, you post a video asking your viewers what your next video should be about. You answer some of their questions in another video, and you give shout-outs to some specific viewers. People like the audience interaction.

Someone in the comments says, "U should pierce your lip! Ud look great!"

That's not something you ever thought about doing. You don't really like the idea of having a pierced lip. But if you do it, you could tease the big day for a couple weeks, then make a video when you get it done. It could be a big boost.

- To pierce your lip, turn to page 41.
- To think of something else to do, turn to page 43.

You need to strike now, while you have all this positive attention. You send an email to the marketing manager of the makeup company. You hear back a few days later. The manager tells you that she has been watching you. She thinks you could be a major influencer one day, but they are not ready to commit to you yet. They want to see you grow your subscriber count.

You need to do something to get their attention. You work hard on a series of posts highlighting fashion and beauty brands that donate part of their profits to good causes. These include supporting domestic violence survivors and working to end homelessness. Your subscribers love the posts. They spread the word about your work on social media.

Your following grows—slowly at first, then rapidly. The makeup company calls back with an offer, and it's good money. You take it. And that's just the beginning! You continue to grow your sponsorships as well as your influence.

People start to think of you as a voice for justice and an authority on health and beauty. You're making good money, and you're making a positive difference while you're doing it. Being a social media influencer is everything you dreamed it would be. It's hard work, but it's definitely the right path for you.

--- THE END ---

To follow another path, turn to page 12.
To learn more about becoming a social media influencer,
turn to page 103.

You decide to wait until you have more followers and subscribers. Then it will be more difficult for the company to say no. So you work harder than ever, blogging and posting almost every day. You get your friends to be in your photo shoots with you and share the photos on their accounts. You blog about the beauty industry and how it can do better to help young people with body image.

You are working almost around the clock. It's hard work. Then one day you make a mistake. You appear in a video wearing jeans—and not the brand that sponsors you. You were so focused on producing content, you forgot this rule. The jeans company cancels their sponsorship, and your income takes a big hit.

You keep making great videos, but without the big sponsor you don't have as much reach. Your follower count flattens out, and you can't find another sponsor. Eventually you decide that being a social media star is not for you.

--- THE END ---

To follow another path, turn to page 12.
To learn more about becoming a social media influencer, turn to page 103.

You decide to give Anna a chance. She might not have managed any huge stars yet, but she still has a strong track record. Plus, Robert says she's good.

It's a great choice. Anna works incredibly hard for you. She gets you two new sponsors right away. She follows trends like a hawk, and she has lots of great ideas for blogging topics.

Your following grows for several weeks. One day, Anna suggests adding more humor to your posts. She helps you come up with some jokes. She even tests some of them out on her friends to find the best ones. Your posts still have quality content, but now they are more entertaining too.

Before long, you have six sponsors, and other companies are begging to be a part of your success. Late night TV hosts even talk about your videos. Eventually, you are asked to be a guest on one of those shows. You're making lots of money, and you're having a good time doing it. Your dream has come true! You're a social media star.

--- THE END ---

To follow another path, turn to page 12.
To learn more about becoming a social media influencer, turn to page 103.

Anna might be good, but you want someone who is great. So you find a more experienced manager through an agency. Jean Paul is very good—he gets you lots of sponsors. But he takes a huge cut of your income. He's also very controlling about what he'll let you post. Instead of being a teammate, Jean Paul is more like a boss.

You grow in popularity, but you're not having fun. You're tired of making money for Jean Paul. One day, you tell him, "I can't do this anymore. You're fired."

You decide to take some time off from social media for a few weeks. You don't even check your feeds to see what others are up to. It feels good to take a break. Who knows? You may never go back to social media.

--- THE END ---

To follow another path, turn to page 12.
To learn more about becoming a social media influencer, turn to page 103.

You do a couple of guest spots on Lexi's video channel. People love them! She continues to be a guest on your channel too. You're both gaining subscribers quickly. In fact, Lexi's follower count grows even higher than yours. You're a little jealous, but you're still having fun.

Then one day, you both get a big break. A TV studio offers you the opportunity to cohost a show about beauty and fashion competitions. You and Lexi will lead competing teams in fashion and beauty challenges. You both accept.

The show is a hit! You and Lexi become TV stars. It's more than you ever dreamed of, and you get to share the experience with your bestie.

--- THE END ---

To follow another path, turn to page 12.
To learn more about becoming a social media influencer, turn to page 103.

You hate to let her down, but you need to focus on your career. She's only doing this for fun, right? "I think we should focus on our own videos for a while," you tell her.

"It's okay," Lexi says. "I totally understand." But you can tell from her voice that she's disappointed.

You post three videos the next week, while Lexi posts four. You have to admit, hers are really good. She's smart, funny, and beautiful. People start subscribing to her channel to see what she'll post next. In fact, her subscriber count soon passes yours.

You try not to feel bad about it and keep working on your own videos. You are doing okay, but Lexi is really hot. After a few months, she calls to tell you some big news. "I'm going to be in this new streaming comedy series called *Moonlighters*," she says.

• Turn the page.

"Oh, Lexi, that's amazing," you manage to say. "Congratulations."

You really are happy for your friend. But you have to admit that you're jealous too. And you're upset with yourself. If only you had teamed up with your friend instead of being so self-involved, you might be having that kind of success now too.

--- THE END ---

To follow another path, turn to page 12.
To learn more about becoming a social media influencer, turn to page 103.

You don't really want to pierce your lip.

But it will help increase your following. You make a video of the piercing, and a lot of your viewers think it's awesome. You get a deal with a local jewelry maker to talk about her products during your videos. You even get a lipstick deal. They love how you talk about applying lipstick and finding shades that work well with your different lip rings. The income from these two sponsors is good. You figure the piercing was worth it.

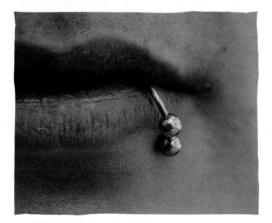

• Turn the page.

At the same time, you're not totally comfortable. It's hard to eat, and you feel like a fake. A pierced lip is not really your style. After a while you take it out. You realize you don't want to act like something you're not just to gain viewers. You decide to take a break from social media for a while. You need to figure out who you really are and what you want to do.

--- THE END ---

To follow another path, turn to page 12.
To learn more about becoming a social media influencer, turn to page 103.

Instead of piercing your lip, you interview people who have lots of piercings. Some have already left comments in your videos. It's a fun series that gets a positive reaction.

But after the excitement of that series wears off, you find yourself in a familiar place. You don't have any ideas for new content. You don't have any sponsors. And you aren't making any money. Your friends and your mom still say you have good beauty tips, but you're just not catching on with a bigger audience. You may not have what it takes to make it big. But the followers you do have are loyal. You'll keep going for them, but you're not going to worry about how often you post or what your subscriber count is. Social media is more fun that way.

--- THE END ---

To follow another path, turn to page 12.
To learn more about becoming a social media influencer, turn to page 103.

DO YOU GET IT?

People have always told you that you're hilarious. And you love making people laugh. You like silly humor, smart humor, and everything in between.

You've spent about a million hours the past couple years watching other people's comedy videos, so you know a little something about how to do it. In fact, you've already made some goofy videos with friends. Now is the time to get serious about being funny.

• Turn the page.

For your first few videos, you create a character you call Mr. Poopsmear. You stage scenes in public places such as parks and malls. Then you come out of a public bathroom with a smear of brown makeup on your cheek. You go on to start conversations with strangers while your friend Robert films from a hidden spot.

Once you get the conversation started, you ask, "Does it smell like poop to you? It smells like I'm still in the bathroom." People don't know that the poop smeared on your face is fake. They usually freak out or react in a funny way. Some try to point it out and give you advice for cleaning up.

Mr. Poopsmear leads to many silly videos, but it gets old fast. You have a good fan base started. But now you need some new material to keep them coming back to your video channel. Do you write a skit, or do you do more public pranks like Mr. Poopsmear?

- To try your hand at skits, turn to page 48.
- To keep doing pranks, turn to page 50.

Getting people to react to goofy behavior
was fun for a while, but you're ready for a new
challenge. Writing and performing skits seems
more creative and fun.

In your first skit, you play a character
who loves jelly—a lot. Grape jelly, peach jelly,
strawberry jelly—you name it. You put it on
everything from toast to hamburgers. You learn
how to make your own jelly. You keep pockets full
of it. Often, you end up with jelly all over your
face and body.

Viewers leave encouraging comments on the
videos. Your loyal subscribers share the videos on
their social media feeds. Slowly but surely, you
gain more subscribers.

You're on a roll. But the skits take a lot of time, creativity, and editing to produce. To succeed as a social media personality, you need to post videos several times a week. There's no way you can keep up that pace writing skits. You need to mix in some easier stuff along with those high-quality skits.

- To read and make fun of online restaurant reviews, turn to page 52.
- To ask your fans to give you a challenge of some kind, turn to page 55.

You've enjoyed getting strangers involved because you never know what someone is going to do or say. The unpredictability is exciting.

So you go to a parking lot at a big-box store. Your friend Robert is filming. You interview people coming out of the store. "If you had to choose between picking your nose in public every hour for the rest of your life or only having one pair of underwear for the rest of your life, which would you choose?" You get some funny conversations. You mix together some of the best reactions into a new video.

Next, you get your brother Jack involved. The two of you start having outrageous arguments in public. "You put nacho cheese in my bed!" "No, I didn't! I put nacho cheese on your bearded dragon. He must have put it in your bed." People walking past give you lots of funny looks.

Some of your videos are hits. Others don't do very well. But you're learning what works and what doesn't. Overall, the team thing is working well, so you decide to permanently team up. Jack wants to do more pranks on people. "Let's do elevator pranks," he says. You were thinking of doing more interviews of people on the street.

- To do elevator pranks, turn to page 56.
- To do interviews on the street, turn to page 58.

You and Robert search for online restaurant reviews that are especially nasty, funny, or ridiculous. You find a couple of restaurants in your area that consistently get bad reviews. You and Robert set up the camera and start reading reviews.

"One time I ate part of a hiking boot on a dare. It was more tender than the steak at this restaurant."

"I'm pretty sure my 'coffee' was brewed with anthill dirt."

"The whole place smells like a milk burp."

You make jokes about how awful these restaurants must be. You joke about how mad one reviewer must have been to go to the trouble to leave his creative, angry review.

The review videos are lots of fun, inexpensive, and quick to make. They also give you a chance to show your real personality instead of a character. And people love them! As your viewers like and share the videos, they climb up the YouTube rankings and get recommended more often.

• Turn the page.

A start-up company that makes stylish hoodies contacts you about a sponsorship. You put their ad at the beginning of your videos, and you start to earn some money. You're ready to make a move to expand your reach.

"You should start a beef with another content creator," Robert says. "You'll be trending like crazy."

You're not sure you want to have a public argument with someone more popular than you. It might be safer to invite another creator to be a guest on one of your videos instead.

- To start a beef, turn to page 60.
- To invite a guest, turn to page 62.

If you're trying to attract new fans, why not ask fans what they want to see? You make a video inviting fans to leave ideas in the comments. "Give me your craziest ideas," you say. "Give me a challenge. What do you want to see me do?"

You get hundreds of ideas in your comments section. Then you make another video where you start to narrow down the list. You finally arrive at two ideas. One is silly—eat a whole pack of veggie burgers as fast as possible. The other is outrageous and illegal—shoplift an easy chair from a furniture store. That video would be epic, but what if you get in trouble?

- To do the veggie-burger challenge, turn to page 64.
- To steal an easy chair, turn to page 66.

Jack insists that his idea for elevator pranks will be hilarious. You reluctantly agree.

You choose an elevator in a professional building with offices on the upper floors. You place two tiny cameras in the corners. Nobody will notice them if they aren't looking for them. Then you wait for someone to get on the elevator on one of the highest floors. You and Jack step in at the same time. On the long ride down, you try to get a reaction from the person. Sometimes you fart. Sometimes you argue with Jack. Sometimes you have outrageous imaginary conversations on your phone. "Emma, I told you to put the body in basement. I'll take care of it when I get home."

After you get a video good enough to keep, you talk to the person in it. You explain that they have been pranked and ask their permission to post the video. Most of them are good sports and agree.

Jack was right! These videos do well with your viewers. So you keep making them. One day, while you're alone in an elevator with a man, you stand very close and whisper in his ear. "Do you have any gum? I had tuna for lunch."

The man is startled and shoves you away. You hit your head on the railing and black out. When you wake up, the man is gone and Jack is there with you. "That. Was. Amazing!" Jack says. "We have to post this right away. It's gold."

You're not so sure. You may have gone too far with this video. Does it make you look funny, or just pathetic? And how could you get the man's permission to post it? You don't know who he is or where he went.

• To post the video, turn to page 68.
• To scrap it, turn to page 69.

You approach people on the street, pretending to be a researcher for a political organization. You start out asking them typical political questions. "Who do you support for president?" Then you add an outrageous question such as, "What do you think about the revelation that the president eats hamsters?" Some people call you out on your ridiculous claim. Others believe you. Some think it's horrible! Others say it's no big deal. One woman says, "That's his business. I don't mind, as long as my taxes stay low."

Your viewership steadily grows. You add advertisements and affiliate links. These links are to products that give you part of the profits if people buy them after clicking from your channel. You even take breaks in the middle of your videos to talk about products that you're paid to talk about. Your viewers don't seem to mind, and the money is good.

You decide you really want to do a TV show. If you were to get on TV, you'd be rich. But you need to become more popular in order to get the attention of TV producers. It's time to get more creative. Do you try something new, like a marathon post? Or do you keep doing public reaction videos, which you already know people like?

- To do a marathon post as a gimmick, turn to page 70.
- To keep doing more public reaction videos, turn to page 72.

There's an influencer who you think really stinks. He has tons of subscribers, and you don't get why. His name is Rocco. You start making fun of him. "All he does is make dumb faces and goofy noises," you say. "For his trademark phrase, he just pulls his hair up and goes, 'Oh my gaaaawd!' It's literally the opposite of funny."

People share your videos, and Rocco notices. He criticizes you back. It's exactly what you wanted. The attention attracts new subscribers for both of you.

You start calling out other creators. You get a reputation for being a jerk. You're a legit star, but you don't like the person you have become.

--- THE END ---

To follow another path, turn to page 12.
To learn more about becoming a social media influencer, turn to page 103.

You invite another comedy content creator named Gina to be a guest in one of your videos. You set it up as a conversation, where you and Gina just talk. You poke fun at some online trends. You laugh at a ridiculous thing a celebrity recently said. You have a great time chatting.

After making the video, you stay in touch with Gina. She's funny and interesting. You support each other's work online. You make a couple more videos with her.

Unfortunately, the videos don't do well. You don't understand why. Some people even leave mean, insulting comments. You lose subscriptions, so you go back to doing skits. But you can't regain the momentum you had before. People just don't seem to think you're that funny anymore.

The good news is that you made a new friend. Gina is great, and the two of you will continue to make the content you love as long as you want to. Maybe someday you'll grab the attention of more people again. Until then, you're still having fun.

--- THE END ---

To follow another path, turn to page 12.
To learn more about becoming a social media influencer, turn to page 103.

At first, you thought the idea of eating a box of 10 veggie burgers on camera was dumb. It's not that funny. But then you realize that it's not about what you do. It's about how you do it. It's up to you to be funny. And you're not crazy about the idea of getting arrested for stealing a chair.

For your veggie-burger challenge video, you decide to do more than just eat burgers. "You guys think I can't eat 10 veggie burgers, huh? Just watch this!"

You cook all 10 burgers and put them in buns. Then you shove them into a blender one at a time. You add some milk to make an enormous veggie-burger smoothie. Then you drink it all in less than five minutes. It is absolutely disgusting. But you throw in a few funny jokes, make lots of gross faces, and eventually get sick. Something about the video catches the attention of some younger fans. They love it. They share it over and over. Pretty soon you are trending nationally.

Then you get an offer from a mobile game company for an ad, but there's a catch. They want you to open your next video by talking about how much you love this game for two full minutes. It's not natural, and you're worried your viewers will know it. You're afraid they'll think you're a fake and a sellout. Of course, it's really good money, so you would be.

- To take the deal, turn to page 73.
- To turn it down, turn to page 74.

This is all in good fun, so it doesn't feel like you're committing a crime. You plan to create a distraction in the furniture store so you and a friend can carry the easy chair out the front door in front of everyone. You have a crew with hidden cameras stationed around the store. They will be able to catch a lot of different angles. It's a crazy idea, but you think you can pull it off.

It all starts when your brother "accidentally" knocks over a shelf of decorative marbles in the back of the store. Employees and security rush to the mess. When they do, you and your friend Robert hoist the chair. It's heavy and awkward. Slowly but surely, you shuffle away with it. You actually get out the door with the chair before security catches up to you.

You spend the night in jail and have to return later to appear in court. The video is really funny. It earns you a lot of clicks and new followers. But later you are sentenced to 30 days in jail. You can't make any videos there. Your subscribers forget about you pretty quickly, and your career takes a nosedive. You have plenty of time in your cell to sit and think about why you did something so dumb just for a few clicks.

--- THE END ---

To follow another path, turn to page 12.
To learn more about becoming a social media influencer, turn to page 103.

After watching the video, you agree that it's funny. You post it and gain more subscribers quickly. You add two new advertisers. You even make T-shirts with the phrase, "Do you have any gum?"

"You have to do more videos like that," Jack says. He thinks you should set up more videos where you offend people. It's dangerous and embarrassing, but you decide to do it anyway.

You make several videos this way. You get pushed and smacked a few times, and you are embarrassed constantly. But you also get rich—people love it. As you sit with an ice pack on your broken nose, you look around at your big new house. Is it worth humiliating yourself for fame and fortune? Most of the time you think it is.

--- THE END ---

To follow another path, turn to page 12.
To learn more about becoming a social media influencer,
turn to page 103.

"I'm not posting that," you tell Jack. "It's ridiculous. Plus that guy could come after me again if I do."

"What's the matter?" Jack asks. "Don't you like being successful?"

But you're not changing your mind. You trash the elevator video and move on to other ideas. Goofy public interviews, prank calls, even a silly song. None of it catches on the way the elevator incident did. Eventually, Jack drops off the team. He says it's no fun anymore, and the money isn't good enough. You agree, but at least you gave it a shot. And you still have some dignity.

--- THE END ---

To follow another path, turn to page 12.
To learn more about becoming a social media influencer, turn to page 103.

You tell your fans that you will livestream 24 hours a day every day for a full week, as long as you keep getting new subscriptions every hour. You ask your subscribers to spread the word and keep new viewers coming in.

Sometimes you are talking a lot to the camera, narrating your day, and working hard to engage your viewers. Other times you're just doing normal things—sleeping, eating, talking to your mom on the phone. People keep watching. You continue gaining new subscribers every hour, so you keep streaming.

Your friends throw a birthday party for another friend, which you attend while recording. They are mildly annoyed at first. After a while, they're really annoyed. You're stealing all the attention from the person whose birthday it is.

"You're always making videos," one of them says. "Can't you stop being an influencer for one afternoon and just be our friend?"

It's a fair question. You've been doing this for so long, playing characters and trying to get reactions out of people, you've lost track of who you really are. Your friends are important to you. You may lose subscribers, but you'd rather lose them than friends. You turn off the camera.

--- THE END ---

To follow another path, turn to page 12.
To learn more about becoming a social media influencer, turn to page 103.

You approach people on the street and ask them how much you would have to pay them to let you shave their head. Someone lets you do it for $100! It's kind of funny, so you do it again. After you get several people to let you shave their heads, you turn the whole thing into a series of videos.

But the videos don't take off. You're not sure why. You need better ideas for content if you're going to be a social media star. But you're not sure you're creative enough. Frustrated and burned out, you decide to give up on becoming a social media influencer.

--- THE END ---

To follow another path, turn to page 12.
To learn more about becoming a social media influencer, turn to page 103.

You do it. You'd be crazy not to accept that kind of money. So at the beginning of your next video, you talk about the game.

Unfortunately, nobody watches the video for more than 30 seconds. They realize it's nothing but a crummy commercial, and they skip to someone else's video. You have to do two more like that to fulfill your contract, and by then everyone thinks you're a phony. Your reputation is in tatters. You may never win back those subscribers.

--- THE END ---

To follow another path, turn to page 12.
To learn more about becoming a social media influencer, turn to page 103.

There's no way you can talk about a game you don't really like for two minutes. Nobody will watch it. Most people will know you're just doing it for the money. One thing you have going for you is that your fans believe you are genuine. You embarrass yourself for them. You put yourself in danger for them. You are never afraid to look ridiculous or take a chance on a weird idea.

You turn down the money. Instead, you keep making funny videos. You get on a roll with really clever, creative skits and commentary. Before long, you get bigger offers from companies that understand who you are. When you start to make good money, you know it's because you stuck to your principles.

--- THE END ---

To follow another path, turn to page 12.
To learn more about becoming a social media influencer,
turn to page 103.

THE VOICE OF A GENERATION

Beauty, fashion, and humor are all interests of yours, but they're not your passion. You've always wanted to be center stage when it comes to singing and performing. Growing up, you often sang for your family. In school, you performed in musicals and sang solos in choir. You started a band with friends, but they weren't as committed as you were. Now is the time to try to make it as a singer by yourself—on social media.

• Turn the page.

You start out by making a couple videos of yourself in your bedroom performing covers of popular songs. It's just you, your guitar, and a camera. You post the videos to several social media platforms. A few friends share them, and a few of their friends share them. They get a decent amount of attention. A handful of strangers comment on them. People say you have a great voice and a charming personality.

You have been writing your own songs for years. Now seems like a good time to record one of them. You're passionate about politics and social issues. In this song, you sing about ocean pollution. This video does even better than the cover songs. Your follower count on Instagram is climbing. You're gaining lots of new subscribers on TikTok and YouTube too. You're even doing well on Twitter, which is not really your thing.

To keep up the momentum, you have to put out content every day. You obviously can't write a new song every day. What else can you do? One idea you have is to do videos where you comment on current events. This would be a way to expand your range of influence from just music. On the other hand, it might make sense to stick to one area—music—and do it well. You could talk about songs and artists.

- To comment on current events, turn to page 80.
- To analyze songs and artists, turn to page 82.

Obviously, you still post plenty of videos of yourself playing guitar and singing. You also post cool selfies. In addition, you do occasional videos and posts about current events. One day, a huge cargo ship gets stuck in a canal in central America. It blocks trade for over a week. This leads you to talk about how corporations only think of profits and never plan for emergencies. Later, a politician is caught breaking a tax law. You call him out.

All the while, your songs get more political. Some people love this new side of you. They grow more passionate as fans. They never miss a post. They share your songs and spread the word about your music. Other people are turned off by the politics. They drop their subscriptions. Some even leave nasty comments or criticize you on social media.

You get the attention of a brand that makes guitar pedals and amps. The company offers you free gear to use in your posts. They are a socially conscious brand with a nonprofit wing that supports voters' rights. You believe in this brand and their cause, so you take the deal. But you need a new song to showcase their gear.

What should you write about? If you keep doing political songs, will people think you're one-dimensional? Maybe you should try something different.

- To write another political song, turn to page 84.
- To try your hand at a love song, turn to page 86.

Over the next couple weeks, you pick three songs that you really love. You make a video about each one. You break down why you think they're great. You talk about lyrics, melodies, bridges, and more. You get deep into this topic, and it's really fun. Your fans enjoy it too.

More importantly, one of the musicians whose song you discuss takes notice. She shares your video on her social media. Suddenly, subscribers start flooding in. You keep doing song-analysis videos, and your popularity continues to grow.

One day you're going through the comments on your YouTube channel. You notice several commenters saying that you're never critical. You only talk about songs you love. And you only say nice things about everyone. They don't think it sounds authentic. "There must be something you don't like!"

Well, there are definitely artists you don't love. You could say a lot about a few songs that really get on your nerves. But you're not crazy about the idea of being critical. It's not like your songs are perfect.

- To do a critical post about a song you don't like, turn to page 87.
- To keep it positive by doing a throwback post about old songs, turn to page 89.

You might as well keep doing what works. You've been toying with a song about a certain politician who says all the right things about fighting climate change. But he keeps voting against real change. He takes donations from a big oil company, and you think he's a hypocrite. You spend a few days tinkering with the song, and pretty soon you think it's good enough to share.

You put on an outfit that makes you look great and set up your usual camera that focuses on the upper part of your body. But you also set up a second camera that's trained on your feet to showcase the new pedals you're using. You record the song, and you edit the video to show the pedals every time you step on them to change sounds.

Your fans love the video. The guitar pedal company loves it too. They buy another package of posts on your Instagram. You reach out to a fashion brand to see if they'd like to sponsor you too. They are a much bigger company than the guitar gear company, and they could bring in more money. But they turn you down. "Sorry," the marketing representative tells you. "You're just too controversial."

You have a good following, but you might not get major brands behind you unless you tone down the politics.

- To pull back on the politics, turn to page 90.
- To stick with politics, turn to page 91.

You're not a one-trick pony! You can sing about lots of things. You write a song comparing love to a dark, smooth lake—underneath the perfect surface, there's a whole world of activity and life that makes it work. It's a beautiful song, maybe your best one yet.

But when you record the song and post the video, it doesn't get the interest that your other songs did. It seems like it doesn't matter how good the song is. You have a reputation as a political protest singer. If you change your tune, people don't know what to make of you. The song flames out, and eventually so do you.

--- THE END ---

To follow another path, turn to page 12.
To learn more about becoming a social media influencer,
turn to page 103.

There's a song that is super popular right now, but you hate it. The autotune is overdone. The structure is a rip-off of an earlier song by another artist. The lyrics are childish. You make a video breaking down everything that doesn't work about the song.

Your video blows up. You get tweets and comments saying things like, "I've always thought this song was overrated but never understood why I hated it so much."

Your critical post makes you more popular than ever, but some of that attention is negative. Some followers are hurt that you basically destroyed one of their favorite songs. But as your popularity has grown, you've started to make good money.

• Turn the page.

After talking with Lexi and Robert, you decide it's time to start selling merch. Lexi thinks you should make a T-shirt that is just your face and logo—a classic, positive design. Robert suggests a T-shirt that has a quote from your review of the song you didn't like. It would be like an inside joke for people who saw the video.

- To make a T-shirt with your face and logo, turn to page 93.
- To make a T-shirt with a mean inside joke, turn to page 94.

You make a video about the top 10 songs the week you were born. You analyze each song and play parts of it. You splice photos of yourself as a baby into the video. It covers lots of music history and some really great songs. Your fans love it.

What now? You need to keep producing content. You have a couple ideas. One is to do an Instagram post about a huge pop star that you admire. If you say something specific and she sees it, she might like or repost it. The traffic this could send your way would be huge.

Your other idea is more of a slow build. You could start a series of videos in which you name "the top 10 greatest songs about friends." You could create lots of content over time and consistently and naturally build your following.

- To post about the pop star, turn to page 96.
- To start the series on songs about friends, turn to page 98.

You want to attract a wider audience, and the political songs are turning off a lot of people. You decide that your new song will be more universal. It's about taking a road trip on a summer day and seeing the countryside. Your song has a catchy chorus, comparing sunshine over a field of wheat to honey.

You post the song, but the reactions are not what you'd hoped. The people who disliked your political songs aren't listening anymore. And your existing fans hate the new song. They were looking for more of what they liked about you in the first place—fierce, socially conscious opinions. Now they think you're a sellout. You should have been more true to yourself.

--- THE END ---

To follow another path, turn to page 12.
To learn more about becoming a social media influencer, turn to page 103.

Taking a stand for what you believe in got you this far. You want to stick with what works. You record a song that criticizes a corporation that is polluting the environment.

It's a huge hit. It racks up countless likes and shares. Eventually, a record label sends you a message. They want to produce all your songs and make an album.

You're thrilled! You go into the studio with a producer, sound technicians, and high-quality recording equipment. It's a big difference compared to recording in your bedroom with the camera and microphone on your laptop!

• Turn the page.

While you're working on the album, you're contacted by Radface Sneakers. This shoe brand wants to play ads on your channel. This would be big money for you, but they want you to sign right away so they can place ads this weekend.

You don't know much about Radface, and you're extremely busy the next few days with recording. You won't have time to research the company. But they probably align with your values, or else why would they ask you? You don't want to miss out on a good opportunity.

- To accept the offer, turn to page 99.
- To tell them you need a few days, turn to page 100.

You think you can sell more T-shirts if the design is more general. Lexi helps you with the design. It shows an outline of your face with your logo on the shoulder. You advertise them on your channel. You talk about them in videos, and wear one in your latest Instagram and TikTok posts.

You sell a lot at first, but then interest dies down. You keep writing and recording songs. Interest from subscribers and advertisers is decent, but it doesn't spike. You can make a living as a social media figure, but you'll probably never be a star. You think you're okay with that.

--- THE END ---

To follow another path, turn to page 12.
To learn more about becoming a social media influencer, turn to page 103.

You can't make a fan out of everyone. But you can give your existing fans a reason to love you more. You decide to make a T-shirt that says, "This lyric is basically a potato." It's an inside joke for anyone who saw your video about the song you hated. Only they will get it. Not everyone will like it, but the people who get it will LOVE it.

And they do. The T-shirts sell out, and you order a second batch. People pop up all over social media wearing "This lyric is basically a potato" T-shirts. That leads more and more people to watch your video. Then they watch other videos of yours, including your own songs. Your reputation is soaring. So are your merch sales and sponsorships.

You keep making posts commenting on music, many of which are snarky and critical. The posts lead to more subscriptions and advertisers. It's a good living, though you don't always feel good about cutting people down for money.

You see many of your fans posting mean things about the artists you criticize. You realize you're contributing to the negativity that you hate on social media. Maybe it's time to rethink being a social media influencer.

--- THE END ---

To follow another path, turn to page 12.
To learn more about becoming a social media influencer, turn to page 103.

You choose a song you really love by Beyonka, a huge pop star, and you learn to play it on your guitar. You record yourself playing it and post the video on YouTube. You post the link on Instagram and hold your breath as you tag her.

Lots of people like and share your post. It gets 10,000 views, but Beyonka doesn't acknowledge it. You do a tribute cover to another star, but this one is less successful than the first one.

You decide to stick to your own music. You get back to work on one of your original songs. You are slowly building a fan base. You're not a star yet, and you might never be. But you are having a great time.

--- THE END ---

To follow another path, turn to page 12.
To learn more about becoming a social media influencer,
turn to page 103.

You start a series of videos playing songs about friends. Then you talk about what you like and don't like about the songs. You also discuss the importance of friends. Each video covers one song. They're a little corny, but people seem to like them. You keep making them, and people start to look forward to your posts.

But after several months, you're still not making enough money to get by. Your following is growing slowly, but you're losing patience. Then, when you finally finish the "songs about friends" series, you have to come up with more content. You enjoy social media, and you love making music for fans. But the constant hustle of being an influencer is exhausting. You never realized how much work it would be. Maybe it's time to consider a different career.

--- THE END ---

To follow another path, turn to page 12.
To learn more about becoming a social media influencer,
turn to page 103.

This is a golden opportunity. You sign the deal with Radface Sneakers. Their ads appear before all your videos. You wear the sneakers during your videos. Your income gets a huge boost, and you really like the shoes. They're comfortable and look hot.

But then someone tweets at you, "Radface factories pour waste into the Yangtze River every day! Shame on you. #radfacepollutes"

You do some quick research online and learn that it's true! Radface is among the worst polluters of all sneaker companies worldwide.

Soon word gets out that you care more about money than the environment. Your reputation is ruined. There's no way to come back from this.

--- THE END ---

To follow another path, turn to page 12.
To learn more about becoming a social media influencer, turn to page 103.

Over the weekend you research Radface Sneakers and find out they are even worse polluters than the other company you spoke out about. They even use child labor! Monday morning, you call back the marketing manager at Radface and tell her no thanks. It's disappointing because you could have made a lot of money. But you have built your reputation on fighting against companies like this.

A few weeks later, you get an offer from a clothing company called WorldThredz that's even better money than the offer from Radface. And they have a great reputation on environmental issues.

Not long after you sign that deal, the studio puts out your album, and it blows up. With WorldThredz backing you, every Instagram post you create brings in $75,000. You can hardly believe how amazing your life has become! You're making great money playing music and posting on social media. You're having a blast, and you're rich. It's hard to believe your dream has really come true.

--- THE END ---

To follow another path, turn to page 12.
To learn more about becoming a social media influencer, turn to page 103.

SOCIAL MEDIA
AS A JOB

Social media is big part of modern life. People use it to stay in touch with family and friends. They use it to learn more about things they care about. They may share jokes, adventures, tunes, feelings, fears, adorable animals, and skateboard tricks. And some people use it to make a living.

A social media influencer is so popular on social media that they can influence what other people buy. They might establish themselves as an authority in a certain area.

To make it as a social media star, you need to figure out how you fit into that world. The choices in this book include fashion and beauty, comedy, and music, but there are as many options as there are people.

Once you find your area, choose the social media channels you want to use. It's good to have a handful that you focus on, such as YouTube, Instagram, TikTok, and Twitch. Match your platforms to the kind of content you want to create. If you are doing videos, you need to be on YouTube or TikTok. If you're doing video games, you'd better be on Twitch.

Figure out what makes you unique, and make content that people will want. Ask yourself the question: Why would anyone follow me? When you're ready to go, you need a plan to produce a lot of content on a regular schedule.

In order to gain followers, your posts need to be frequent and good. It is a lot of work. While you're at it, make sure you're connecting with other influencers on your platforms. Make relationships and build a community. Reach out to brands in your area of interest.

So how do you make money? If you have enough followers, brands will be interested in you. They may pay you to advertise their products on your channels, talk about their products, or post links to their website. That's because the people who follow you trust you. They are more likely to buy the products you recommend.

Being a social media influencer isn't just fun and photos. It's hard work to produce content and manage all your profiles. For many, it can be overwhelming. For others, it's a perfect fit.

SOCIAL MEDIA STAR
FAME OR FORTUNE
REALITY CHECK

Mega influencers are people with at least 1 million followers on at least one platform. Many mega influencers are movie stars, athletes, and musicians. Major brands might pay them $1 million per post.

It's important for brands to match up with the right influencer. A rock musician would be a great influencer for a brand of headphones but probably not real estate.

WANT TO KNOW WHERE YOUR FAVORITE SOCIAL NETWORK RANKS WORLDWIDE?

As of September 2021, the following sites had this many active users:

YouTube: 2.291 billion

WhatsApp: 2 billion

Instagram: 1.386 billion

TikTok: 732 million

Snapchat: 514 million

Are you curious how many subscribers some of your favorite YouTubers have?

MattyBRaps: 14.2 million subscribers

Its JoJo Siwa: 12.3 million subscribers

Brooklyn and Bailey: 6.91 million subscribers

Johnny Orlando: 4.61 million subscribers

Jacob Sartorius: 3 million subscribers

OTHER PATHS TO EXPLORE

What type of social media influencer would you like to be? Which platform would you like to focus on and why?

Imagine an advertiser offers to pay you a lot of money to say good things on your social media about their product—but you really don't like that product. How do you handle this? What are the pros and cons of taking the deal?

What qualities are most important in making a social media star successful? Why do you think those are the most important?

GLOSSARY

affiliate link (uh-FIL-ee-uht LINK)—a hyperlink to an advertiser's website that if someone clicks it, the advertiser knows that the person came to their website from the affiliate's website

blog (BLOG)—an online journal that is updated regularly; short for "web log"

content (KAHN-tent)—material, such as videos, photos, written words, and audio, that is produced and offered on a website such as a social media platform

influencer (IN-floo-uhnss-ur)—a person who is able to inspire or guide interest in something, especially to purchase something

livestream (LIVE-streem)—to broadcast an event live over the internet

platform (PLAT-fohrm)—an application or website that allows people to use a service, such as a type of social media

subscriber (suhb-SKRIBE-uhr)—a person who signs up to receive content from a person or organization, sometimes for a fee

SELECT BIBLIOGRAPHY

Forbes: How to Become a Social Media Influencer in Ten Simple Steps
forbes.com/sites/quora/2017/05/25/how-to-become-a-social-media-influencer-in-ten-simple-steps/

How to Become an Influencer: 7 Easy Steps to Becoming a Social Media Influencer Today
influencermarketinghub.com/how-to-become-an-influencer/

READ MORE

Dell, Pamela. *Understanding Social Media*. North Mankato, MN: Capstone Press, 2020.

Juilly, Brett. *Make Your Own Amazing YouTube Videos: Learn How to Film, Edit, and Upload Quality Videos to YouTube*. New York: Racehorse for Young Readers, 2017.

McKee, Jonathan. *The Teen's Guide to Social Media . . . & Mobile Devices: 21 Tips to Wise Posting in an Insecure World*. Uhrichsville, OH: Shiloh Run Press, 2017.

INTERNET SITES

A Day in the Life of a Fashion Blogger
youtube.com/watch?v=VwCN1-MPCmw

Protecting Your Online Identity and Reputation
kidshealth.org/en/teens/online-id.html?WT.ac=t-ra

WatchMojo.com: Top 10 Funniest YouTube Channels
youtube.com/watch?v=D9izhgsToYg

ABOUT THE AUTHOR

Eric Braun is a children's author and editor.
He has written dozens of books on many topics,
and one of his books was read by an astronaut on
the International Space Station for kids on Earth to
watch. Eric lives in Minneapolis with his wife, two
kids, and a dog who is afraid of cardboard.